4

INVESTMENT TIPS FOR STUDENTS

A guide to making wise financial decisions as a student

Leon Rowe

AF445854

Copyright©2022 Leon Rowe

All Rights Reserved

TABLE OF CONTENTS

INTRODUCTION

The moment is now to start making stock market investments, even if you're still in college. Why? Because the earlier you start investing, the greater your prospects are of accumulating large wealth over the long term. But if you're a complete novice, the prospect of investing might be really terrifying. And up until the coronavirus crisis, it undoubtedly appeared that saving for the future was something that only the wealthy or those who were getting ready for retirement did. College students are not too young to begin investing, despite popular assumption. Yes, I am referring about investing in students. The majority of individuals are unaware of the value of investments for students. In actuality, college students who start investing now are positioning themselves for a lifetime of wealth accumulation. Not many students are in a position to invest, but doing so while still in school or with the advantage of not having to take out loans is a wise move. Students need to understand that while saving is the prudent course of action, investing in little amounts enables the money to grow on its own. Everything you need to know about the value of early investing as a student is addressed in this book.

CHAPTER 1

WHY SHOULD YOU INVEST AS A STUDENT?

Early investing enables you to develop disciplined spending habits by keeping an eye on your budget and making the required changes to your expenditure. Here, the objective is to earn money through saving. This is just another aspect of the advantages of investing for students.

This is not possible with poor spending habits and a life full of impulsive purchases. The lessons you acquire through student investing will benefit out in the long run, especially when you have more money to manage and discipline is needed. The biggest returns on money are often achieved by more variable investments. Investors with the time to recover from a bad situation may choose to make riskier bets. Traditional college students in their 20s have an advantage when it comes to investing because of time. Typically, they can make up for any potential losses in due course. It can be scary to learn the ins and outs of the market, but a college student's willingness to take chances can help them get past that barrier. When investing, college students frequently approach it with the mindset that they have nothing to lose. Although dangerous for the majority of investors, this mindset can allow students to get practical market knowledge before they reach the real world. People who start investing later in life are frequently by nature more careful with their financial decisions. The more likely you are to comprehend the value of investment and the better off you will be financially in the long run, the sooner you start investing. Over time, you will be able to purchase items that others cannot, unlike your peers who may have opted to invest later in life. Additionally, your finances might at some point become unstable, but by starting your investments early, you'll be ready to handle these difficulties. I hope you now realize how crucial investments are for students. In most cases, financial independence is a skill that is not taught in college. You often start learning how to manage your money on your own when you acquire your first job. Why wait much longer to begin? Beginning with student investments can assist college students in learning how to conduct financial research, decipher a balance sheet, and evaluate risk. A student could develop a sense of pride in their financial future by taking an active role in their investing. This means that for students, investing is crucial.

CHAPTER 2

TIP 1 – CHOOSE YOUR INVESTMENTS PROPERLY

It might be a little overwhelming to decide which stocks, shares, or funds to purchase, especially if you're new to investing. However, here is where the study comes into play. Always make sure you are familiar with your investments. It doesn't necessarily follow that something said on Twitter about a certain stock being a smart investment is real.

The stock market offers a variety of investing opportunities. You have two options for investing: either buy index funds or shares of particular companies, which is a more hands-on strategy (such as the S&P 500 or FTSE 100). A set of equities or bonds are tracked by index funds. Examples are the S&P 500, which tracks the top 500 US companies, and the FTSE 100, which tracks the top 100 UK companies. You can invest in an index fund as opposed to having to acquire one share of each firm, which would be incredibly costly and time-consuming. It's sometimes thought of as a simple and risk-free method of investing because your money is dispersed across numerous businesses. The best method to reduce risk in your portfolio is through diversification. You can achieve this through investing in index funds as well as by diversifying your portfolio across several markets, regions, and industries. You will have additional businesses and markets to offset any losses if one company or market's worth declines.

You Can Invest In:

1) Bonds
2) Mutual funds
3) Stocks
4) Target date funds

BONDS

You are essentially lending money to a business or the government when you purchase a bond. You will receive the money you lent them back along with interest income in return at a later time. Purchasing bonds won't yield as much profit as investing in equities or index funds, for example. However, they are regarded as low-risk assets, which makes them crucial to have in order to balance your investment portfolio and reduce risk.

MUTUAL FUNDS

Mutual funds are frequently a smart place to start for novice investors. This is so that a professional fund manager can invest in a variety of assets using a pool of investor cash that you contribute to when you purchase mutual funds.

Additionally, the skilled fund managers handle all significant investment choices on your behalf at no additional charge. In other words, you obtain a balanced investment with mutual funds. And in contrast to buying individual stocks, you don't have to put in as much effort or assume as much risk to get that.

STOCKS

You can acquire a small portion of a corporation by buying a stock. Ideally, as the value of the business rises over time, so will the value of your little stake in it. Of course, there is no guarantee of that. Additionally, the company's value can decline following your stock purchase; this happens frequently.

Furthermore, it might be challenging to choose the correct companies to invest in. However, stock investment is where you'll make the most money if you can do it correctly. Later on in this piece, we also provide advice on how to do it.

TARGET DATE FUNDS

Another kind of mutual fund that owns a mix of equities and bonds is a target-date fund. A target-date fund allows you to automatically invest with a particular end date in mind (e.g.

retirement). Your investments will gradually become more cautious as that date draws closer in order to reduce potential risk. When considering your long-term financial objectives, this is a smart investment choice.

.

CHAPTER 3

TIP 2 – CONTROL YOUR RISK

Everyday dangers are present. Suppose you go to the grocery store or to work by car. The possibility of a crash exists at all times. Working from home or eating delivery could completely eliminate that risk. Wearing a seat belt and utilizing defensive driving techniques could help you reduce that danger. The danger could also be transferred by using a vehicle service or public transportation.

The same is true of financial risks, such as the loss risk you assume while investing, the value of your investments being depreciated by inflation, or the possibility that you won't have enough money to support yourself in retirement. You can prevent some of these dangers. You must control others. Of course, each path has benefits and drawbacks. But being aware of this structure can help you make wiser financial decisions.
Emotional and monetary factors both play into risk capacity. For example, even if you have more than enough money to retire, you might not be mentally prepared to face the chance of living solely off of your savings. If you lack

sufficient savings, you can be emotionally prepared to act, but you lack the necessary funds. You are a low-risk person in both scenarios. However, you might also be financially and emotionally prepared. You can accept high risk in this situation.

Even if you have no influence over how the stock market will act, you might be able to reduce your chance of losing money by making certain investments. Additionally, the investment products and accounts you select might help you reduce the taxes and fees you pay.

<u>HOW YOU CAN CONTROL RISK</u>

1) **Apportionment of assets:** In the past, stocks have generally delivered higher returns while also carrying higher risk than bonds. Setting a mix of stocks, bonds, and short-term assets that is in line with your time horizon for investing, your financial needs, and your comfort level with volatility is a crucial step in managing investment risk.

2) **Identification of assets:** By holding highly taxed investments, such as bonds, stocks held for a year or less, and real estate investment trust funds (REITs), in 401(k)s and IRAs (if your plan offers them), you may be able to reduce your federal income taxes. Conversely, you should leave investments taxed at relatively low capital gains rates in taxable brokerage accounts. Tax reductions can hasten the growth of your money.

CHAPTER 4

TIP 3 – ACQUIRE ADEQUATE KNOWLEDGE

Thanks to the internet, finding information on any topic is now simpler than ever. You could easily see people's eyes glued to their phone screens if you were out in public and looked around. The constant onslaught of irrelevant information makes it extremely difficult to focus on the vital things, therefore this benefit has also been a hardship.

Most of us have books or articles lying around that we've been wanting to read for years but haven't since it's so difficult to stay up to date in the digital age. The majority of the time, it may be difficult to tell which information source to believe. Although increasing your investment knowledge is a challenging endeavor, if you have a clear goal, form the proper habits, and adhere to them over time, you will improve as a person.

If you keep feeding your brain, knowledge will accumulate gradually, but you must realize that disposition isn't enough to succeed; the most important thing is for you to sustain a high degree of curiosity for a long period.

You can acquire investment knowledge through:

- Reading market updates on reputable websites and blogs on a daily or monthly basis

- Reading of quarterly and annual reports from businesses and sectors.

- Reading financial journals and business magazines. Numerous reports are available for free download on the websites of some financial institutions.

- Read primary data more often than secondary data.

- Stream investing and finance-related podcasts.

- Read literature and research investing's past. Learn about market bubbles, the reasons why markets rise and fall, and the characteristics of recessions and depressions.

CHAPTER 5

TIP 4 – HAVE A BUDGET

Your monthly income and costs are listed in your spending plan, sometimes referred to as your budget. It can assist you in determining how much money is being used for both necessary and discretionary expenses, and you can then make changes as necessary. Your budget needs to take both recurring and one-time spending into consideration. The cost of the securities determines how much money is spent for a single share. (Share values can range from a few pennies to several thousands of dollars.)

Although capital investment is rife with sophisticated strategies and techniques, some of the most active investors have done little more than follow the fundamentals of the stock market.

When you begin investing in stocks or mutual funds, the hardest thing to do is to refrain from looking at them. It's vital to avoid falling into the trap of testing your stocks frequently throughout the day, every day, if you want to beat the odds and succeed at day trading.

You also don't want to remain completely passive, though. Your investing strategy needs to be evaluated on a regular basis to see whether there is opportunity for improvement. So just add a reminder on your calendar to check your accounts periodically. When you first start out, once a month or every other month is sufficient. It's crucial to develop good money management skills as you start college and try to balance work and studies. If not, you can have some unwelcome surprises at the conclusion of the semester. Budgeting is so crucial for college students.

Budgeting may seem like it would take the fun out of living, but it's crucial to have a clear grasp of your financial situation. You can work towards your financial objectives using a budget. The costs of living may not be too high when you are a college student. However, when you factor in costs associated with attending college, your budget for students needs to accommodate considerably more. So, while you plan your expenditures, keep the following expenses in mind. It is imperative that you keep track of your spending. You'll have a better understanding of where your money is going if you keep diligent track of your costs. If you are unhappy with your present spending, changing your spending habits will allow you to track your improvement.

CONCLUSION

Do you believe you need a certain amount of money to begin investing? $500? $10,000? $20,000? Well you are correct, of course. But a lot less is all you really need to get started. Exactly how much? $10 to $20 per month. Seriously. You can get started with just that. Without a doubt, you'll need more if you wish to be very wealthy. However, a few no-fee online brokers, and micro-investing applications make it possible to get started with a very small investment. Use the tips given in this book and apply it with your little funds and you'll be shocked by the results. Now more than ever, investing on a budget has never been simpler. If you want to become an expert investor, you have a lot to understand. Fortunately, you don't need to be an expert to start. Even if you're a college student with not much money to spare, you can get started right away! I hope the knowledge I've provided here enables you to accomplish that.

www.ingramcontent.com/pod-product-compliance
Lightning Source LLC
Chambersburg PA
CBHW080945120726
48003CB00011B/3304